GLOW IN THE DARK:
NATURE'S LIGHT
SPECTACULAR

written by
KATY FLINT

illustrated by
CORNELIA LI

WIDE EYED EDITIONS

Meteor showers are named after the star constellation from where they appear to fall. The Perseid meteor shower is named after the Perseus constellation.

The best time to see them is after midnight, in a dark, open space, away from city lights, trees, and buildings.

METEOR SHOWERS

CASE STUDY: MERCANTOUR NATIONAL PARK, FRANCE

Nature puts on the most amazing natural fireworks, if you just know where to look. Start by gazing up at the stars in your own backyard or local green space. For many months of the year, meteor showers can be seen with just your eyes. Look for their streaking tails as they shoot across the sky. Meteors are actually space rocks falling to Earth. They fall so fast that they heat up the air and leave a glowing tail behind them. This is why they are sometimes called shooting stars, even though meteors are not stars. When a group of meteors fall together, we call it a meteor shower.

WHAT'S HAPPENING?

Atmosphere

Streaks of light as space rock burns up

Earth

Meteors

Meteors range in size from a speck of dust to the size of a pebble or a boulder. Most meteors are not much bigger than a speck of sand. And most burn up before they get to Earth.

We get meteor showers when planet Earth passes through a cloud of dust and space rock.

In history, eclipses used to scare people as they didn't know the science behind what was happening. They thought this natural phenomenon was something supernatural.

The Sun is 400 times wider than the Moon, but it is also 400 times further away than the Moon. Therefore, the two look nearly the same size from Earth.

SOLAR ECLIPSE

CASE STUDY: SUN VALLEY, IDAHO, USA

If day suddenly plunges into darkness, you are probably experiencing a cosmic event known as a solar eclipse. A solar eclipse happens when the Moon travels in between the Sun and Earth. The Moon blocks the Sun's rays, and casts a shadow onto parts of the Earth for a few minutes. As our planet spins round, different places on Earth fall under the Moon's shadow. This moving area of full shadow is called the "Path of Totality." People in this path see a total eclipse, with the Sun completely blocked out. Everyone else might see a partial eclipse, or nothing... Total eclipses happen approximately every 18 months somewhere on Earth.

WHAT'S HAPPENING?

Sun

Moon

Partial eclipse

Earth

Total eclipse

Partial eclipse

Animals and plants can respond differently to an eclipse. Birds may stop chirping, bees stop buzzing, and flowers may close up.

You should never look directly at the Sun—even during an eclipse, even with sunglasses. It will damage your eyesight forever. Ask an adult to find special solar viewing glasses you can wear to watch an eclipse.

DOUBLE RAINBOWS

CASE STUDY: LAKE DISTRICT, ENGLAND

Rainbows are created by reflection (bouncing) and refraction (bending) of light in water droplets, which cause a spectrum of colored light to appear. Double rainbows happen when light is reflected twice within a raindrop.

WHAT'S HAPPENING?

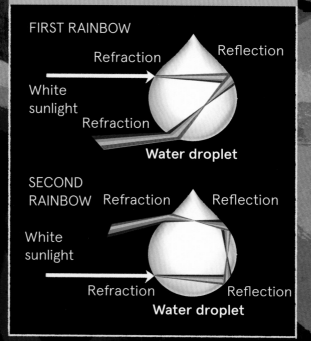

FIRST RAINBOW

Refraction   Reflection

White
sunlight

Refraction

Water droplet

SECOND
RAINBOW   Refraction   Reflection

White
sunlight

Refraction   Reflection

Water droplet

The reflection and refraction for single and double rainbows happens in the same raindrop. However, our eyes see different colors from different raindrops.

If you are outside on a sunshine-and-showers kind of day, you might be lucky enough to see a rainbow—or even a double rainbow. Rainbows happen when light strikes falling water droplets. The water droplets make the hidden colors in sunlight spread out so you can see each color separately. A multicolored arc appears in the sky, displaying a spectrum of colors ordered red, orange, yellow, green, blue, indigo and violet. A double rainbow is where two arcs can be seen in the sky at once. The second rainbow's colors are paler, and in the opposite order to the first: violet, indigo, blue, green, yellow, orange, and red. Look out for one next time it rains.

A rainbow is not an object, so unfortunately you cannot find it and touch it.

You will have most likely seen rainbows in the rain. They can also be seen in mist, fog, and dew, whenever there are water droplets in the air and light shining at the right angle.

You can create your own rainbows by spraying mist from a hose in the backyard on a sunny day. It's best to do this when the Sun is low in the sky and when you are standing with your back to the Sun.

VOLCANIC LIGHTNING

CASE STUDY: CALBUCO VOLCANO, CHILE

Sometimes when something looks amazing in nature, it can also be very dangerous. This is the case with volcanic lightning —also known as a dirty thunderstorm. Particles of ash explode from the volcano, filling the sky with thick clouds, where they rub against each other and become charged with electricity. These charged particles generate sparks of lightning, which tear through the ash clouds, releasing some of the huge amounts of electricity building up above the erupting volcano. SPARK AND FLASH!

After years of inactivity, this volcano has burst into life. It has brought planes to a standstill and people have had to be evacuated for safety.

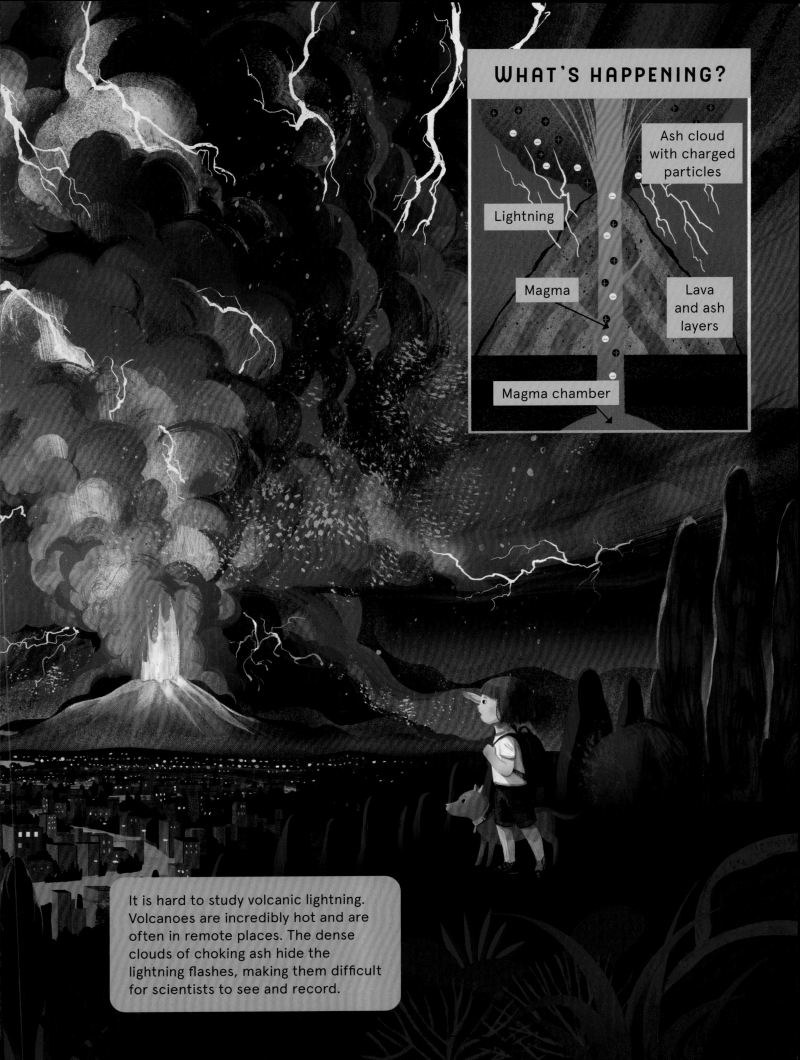

WHAT'S HAPPENING?

Ash cloud with charged particles

Lightning

Magma

Lava and ash layers

Magma chamber

It is hard to study volcanic lightning. Volcanoes are incredibly hot and are often in remote places. The dense clouds of choking ash hide the lightning flashes, making them difficult for scientists to see and record.

THE POLAR LIGHTS

CASE STUDY: SVALBARD, NORWAY

"Aurora" means "goddess of the dawn."

The auroras have confused many people throughout history. Vikings thought they were caused by the shining weapons of immortal warriors.

You can watch the most spectacular light displays at the North and South Poles. Many explorers trek across harsh conditions to get a glimpse of the strange magnetic movements that dance across the sky. They are the *Aurora Australis* (southern lights) around the South pole, and the *Aurora Borealis* (northern lights) around the North pole, which you can see here. The auroras are caused by solar wind crashing into Earth's magnetic field. This disturbance makes charged particles trapped in the magnetic field whizz around at high speeds. The particles hit gases high in the sky, causing them to glow with the ghostly colors of the auroras. This is strongest—and most visible—at the Arctic and Antarctic Circles.

Which colors you see all depends on which gases the particles crash into. Oxygen gives off green or red, and nitrogen gives off blue and purple. If all the colors mix together, they appear as white or dim light.

The magical glow comes from charged particles in the area of space around the Earth hitting gases and making them give off light.

There is always an aurora happening somewhere on Earth—even in the daytime. You have to have the right weather conditions and amount of darkness to see them.

WHAT'S HAPPENING?

Solar winds

Particles zooming down towards the poles

Earth

SUPER BLOOD MOON

CASE STUDY: ATHENS, GREECE

A super blood moon happens just before a lunar eclipse. Lunar means "moon" and "eclipse" means to block out (read about solar eclipses on page 4). In a lunar eclipse, Earth blocks sunlight from reaching the Moon. A total lunar eclipse happens when the Moon passes exactly behind the Earth so that the Sun, Moon, and Earth become (more or less) in line with each other. The only light that reaches the Moon is the long wavelengths of red light stretching around the edges of the Earth's atmosphere. Despite its name, and fiery red glow, there is nothing to worry about. Super moons happen fairly frequently and are not a sign of anything scary.

The Moon normally looks a bright silvery gray color to us because it reflects the Sun's light against the dark night sky. In fact, it's the color of charcoal, or asphalt.

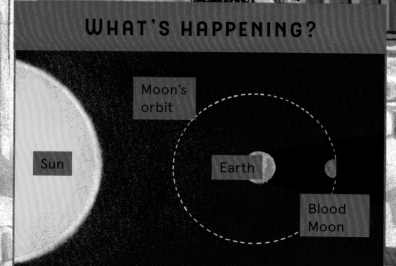

WHAT'S HAPPENING?

Sun

Moon's orbit

Earth

Blood Moon

FIREFALL

CASE STUDY: YOSEMITE, CALIFORNIA, USA

Firefall season at Yosemite National Park is something mythical to behold. Every February, you can see the waterfall over El Capitan light up in the rays of the setting sun and overflow like red-hot lava. Conditions must be right: clear skies, perfect timing, and cold enough for it to have snowed—but warm enough for the snow to melt during the day. If the setting Sun is in the right spot of the western sky, it will illuminate the waterfall with its winter rays. The phenomenon only lasts about 10 minutes so you have to be ready and waiting in the exact place to catch it. It is incredibly popular and thousands of visitors flock each year to catch a glimpse and take a photo.

VIEWING AREA MAP

Horsetail Fall

Viewing and picnic area

LIGHT PILLARS

CASE STUDY: ONTARIO, CANADA

Ice crystals normally stay at cloud level. But when they sink lower, they can also be called crystal fog, or DIAMOND DUST, because of the way they bend light. You can feel them on your skin.

WHAT'S HAPPENING?

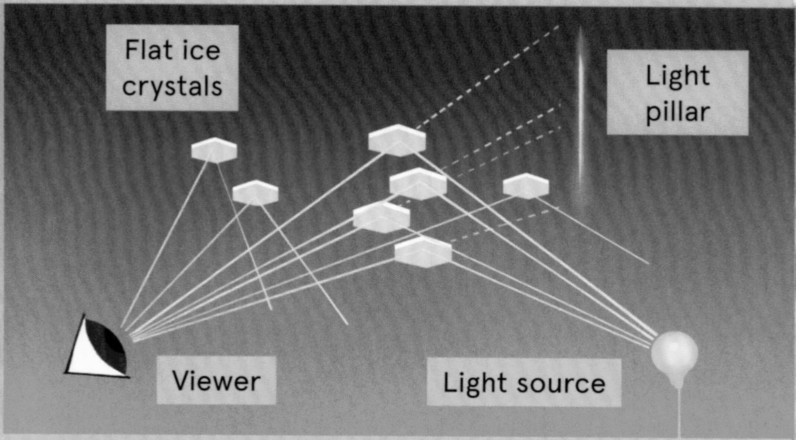

Flat ice crystals

Light pillar

Viewer

Light source

Your eyes see a light pillar in the sky beyond the crystals.

The temperature has to be BELOW ZERO in order to create a light pillar.

Light pillars can also be created by moonlight or sunlight, as well as artificial light.

While the beams may look beautiful, they are sadly a sign of LIGHT POLLUTION.

What may look like alien beams, or lasers, in the sky, is actually what happens when millions of tiny, plate-like ice crystals reflect (bounce) the light from streetlights downwards into your eyes. So don't panic or report them as UFOs! The reflections from the ice crystals create an optical illusion in which you appear to see tall shafts of light shooting upwards into the night sky. The crystals that produce the light pillars are about halfway between you and the streetlights. You are more likely to see light pillars on a winter's night, when the cold air causes the flat ice crystals to sink lower to the ground. Ice crystals can cause other light phenomena in the daytime, like the sundogs on the next page.

SUNDOGS

CASE STUDY: THEODORE ROOSEVELT NATIONAL PARK, NORTH DAKOTA, USA

The same phenomenon can also happen with moonlight—then we call them MOONDOGS.

The ice crystals are hexagonally shaped.

When the Sun nears the horizon, bright, angelic shapes can appear like a halo. These shapes are known as sundogs, and are caused by ice crystals, which scatter light at high altitudes like prisms. Photographers take amazing shots of this through their camera lenses. Sundogs can often have a rainbow effect, where the light has been spread out into the color order we talked about earlier on: red, orange, yellow, green, blue, indigo, and violet. A good way to remember this order is to imagine a person called Roy G. Biv, or say the phrase "Richard Of York Gave Battle In Vain" out loud.

WHAT'S HAPPENING?

Glowworms lying in a silk hammock

Sticky threads up close

Glowworms are not worms but the LARVAE (grubs) of a fungus gnat fly (similar to a mosquito.) The larvae are only the size of a matchstick.

A MAORI CHIEF named Tane Tinorau originally explored this cave in 1887.

There are eels in the water so don't go for a swim.

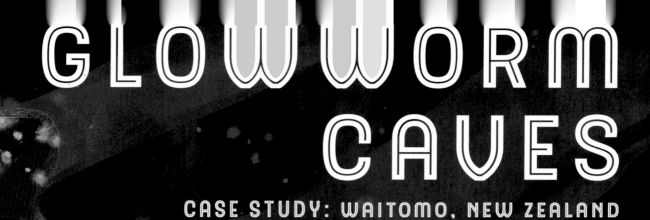

GLOWWORM CAVES

CASE STUDY: WAITOMO, NEW ZEALAND

The caves here are 30 million years old!

The species of glowworm in this cave is called *Arachnocampa luminosa* and is only found in New Zealand.

Sailing into Waitomo's glowworm caves, you might think that there were fairy lights strung from every ripple in the rock formation. These tiny bright lights are powered by thousands of glowworms, which produce light in their tails. This kind of living light, called bioluminescence, attracts unsuspecting insects into their tangle of sticky silk threads. Bioluminescent animals make light by way of a reaction in their bodies, between oxygen and light-producing chemicals. You might know some other bioluminescent animals already, such as deep sea fish or jellyfish.

The rainbow halo around the shadow is called a "GLORY." This is most commonly seen by people in an airplane, when they spot a shadow and rainbow beneath them in the clouds.

The name is said to have come from the BROCKEN PEAK in the Harz Mountains in Germany, where the story goes that a climber was so frightened by the illusion he fell to his death. So be careful!

If you are ever walking in high mountains among fog and mist, you may see what looks like another giant person walking in front of you. Surprise—it's actually you! Or, your shadow to be exact. The Sun shining behind you can cast a shadow through the fog, which looks like someone moving in the distance. If the shadow moves, shifts or distorts it could be because of water droplets in the air. Your eyes are playing tricks on you!

BROCKEN SPECTRE

CASE STUDY: MOUNT EMEI, CHINA

The rainbow comes from light being refracted (bent) in the water droplets of the mist, like we learned on page 6.

In history, people thought that seeing this halo made them special, or saintly.

WHAT'S HAPPENING?

Sun

Person standing above

Mist

Shadow

Brimming with creative inspiration, how-to projects, and useful information to enrich your everyday life, Quarto Knows is a favourite destination for those pursuing their interests and passions. Visit our site and dig deeper with our books into your area of interest: Quarto Creates, Quarto Cooks, Quarto Homes, Quarto Lives, Quarto Drives, Quarto Explores, Quarto Gifts, or Quarto Kids.

Glow in the Dark: Nature's Light Spectacular © 2020 Quarto Publishing plc.
Illustrations by Cornelia Li. Written by Katy Flint.
Natural history consultation by Barbara Taylor.

First Published in 2020 by Wide Eyed Editions, an imprint of The Quarto Group.
100 Cummings Center, Suite 265D, Beverly, MA 01915 USA.
T +1 978-282-9590 F +1 978-283-2742 **www.QuartoKnows.com**

A catalogue record for this book is available from the British Library.

ISBN 978-0-7112-5197-7

The illustrations were created digitally using hand-painted textures.
Set in Hipton Sans, Roboto Slab, and Apercu.

Published by Georgia Amson-Bradshaw
Designed by Karissa Santos
Production by Chris Tucker
Manufactured in Guangdong, China CC122019
9 8 7 6 5 4 3 2 1